THE FRONT
~ PORCH ~

THE FRONT
~ PORCH ~

—— Ann Rooney Heuer ——

Barnes & Noble Books
Books
NEW YORK

Dedication

For my husband, Frederick, and our daughter, Marlene; for my parents, Elizabeth and Francis; for my sister Ellen; and for my two talented editors, Francine Hornberger and Reka Simonsen. These guiding lights inspire me to take the road less traveled to write about things bright and beautiful.

A BARNES & NOBLE BOOK

First Barnes & Noble Edition 2002

©1998 Michael Friedman Publishing Group, Inc.

ISBN 0-7607-4111-5

Editors: Francine Hornberger and Reka Simonsen
Art Director: Jeff Batzli
Designer: Jennifer S. Markson
Photography Editor: Sarah Storey
Production Manager: Camille Lee

Color separations by Fine Arts Repro House Co., Ltd.
Printed in China by C.S. Graphics Shanghai Co., Ltd.

3 5 7 9 10 8 6 4

TABLE OF CONTENTS

INTRODUCTION

"Why do we love certain houses, and why do they seem to love us? It is the warmth of our individual hearts reflected in our surroundings."

—T.H. Robsjohn-Gibbings

With its promise of blue sky days and starry nights, summer is the season when we trade the cocoon of our homes for the freedom and comforts of the front porch. Serving as a breezy family room, a neighborly gathering spot, an al fresco dining room, or a hobby room, the front porch is a favorite place to celebrate the pleasures of life. For the young and for those rich in years, it can become the heart of the home from late spring through Indian summer.

Originating in Ancient Greece, the front porch has been a prominent feature of many homes since colonial times. In the 1700s, European-inspired porches were a necessity of life in sultry southern climes. By the mid-1800s, families everywhere enjoyed "sitting a spell" on their front porches. In fact, during the Victorian era (1837–1901) when a well-dressed home announced one's place in society, decorative front porches were essential. Following World War II, however, the front porch and its tradition of hospitality began to fade into history. Many old houses were torn down to make room for easy-maintenance modern homes. Many families now spent summer nights on the new backyard patio, inside the house watching TV, or at the drive-in movie theater.

It's been said that "everything old is new again" and happily, the faithful front porch is once again in vogue as people seek to improve the quality of their homes—and their lives.

One of the many benefits of this outdoor living space involves energy conservation. The sheltering front porch averts the intense heat of the sun, creating a cool spot for gathering in the home, and thus, cutting air-conditioning costs. Also, for sheer curb appeal, the front porch adds dimension and a sense of character to a home's exterior.

Dennis A. Andrejko, AIA, Chairman of the School of Architecture and Planning at the State University of New York at Buffalo says, "Symbolically, front porches send a message to the public about the need for community interaction and people opening up to one another. In this age of

Opposite: THIS ELEGANT FRONT PORCH AFFORDS A WONDERFUL VIEW OF THE LUSH GREENERY AND VIBRANT FLOWERS SURROUNDING THE HOUSE.

cookie-cutter style neighborhoods, many people want their homes to make a unique statement through the amenity of the front porch."

It's no wonder then, that updating an existing structure or building a new front porch are popular home improvement projects. It's also common for homeowners to convert an open front porch into a screened porch to keep insects at bay and to make the room inviting for dining and sleeping. An exciting new innovation that meets the needs of all climates is the convertible porch, which can be adjusted to serve as an open, screened, or totally enclosed porch with glazed inserts. Also, some homeowners opt to enjoy the comforts of year-round porch living by converting the porch into a sunroom or by adding a conservatory. A century ago, Victorian conservatories were the perfect setting for exotic plants and declarations of love.

If you're thinking about building or renovating a front porch or you're considering extending your living space with a conservatory, it's vital to do some research. Books and magazines on home design and remodeling can help you learn how to enhance your home's facade while maintaining its original lines. Consulting with several contractors regarding the project is also an informative step.

Contractor Gary Reid, founder of Gary Reid Construction, Inc. of Youngstown, New York says, "If your home has a front porch, it's important to realize that structural problems can occur in several places. An experienced contractor can check for deterioration in the foundation,

support posts, floor joists, and the roof support structures, and can make any necessary repairs."

Reid notes that people in the forest industry have published numerous articles about which woods are best for porch and deck construction. Superior woods include Atlantic White Cedar, Redwood, and Western Red Cedar. Each of these has a natural immunity system that helps it to survive moisture and insect infestation. Reid recommends properly treating these durable woods with a penetrating wood preservative followed by a coat of latex or oil primed mildewstat resistant sealer. If a painted finish is desired, two top coats of all acrylic latex paint can then be applied.

Without question, a front porch adds charisma to a home's facade when careful consideration is given to key elements of design, such as paint, lighting, window and floor treatments, furnishings, and accessories. This volume will tour dozens of beautiful homes where front porch personality is formal or fanciful, in touch with nature or in step with the past.

First are the Romantic homes popular in the nineteenth century—Greek Revival, Gothic Revival, and Italianate. In this chapter,you will discover the unique possibilities these styles present in traditional porch decor. The next chapter features Victorian homes with lacy verandas, sleeping porches, and conservatories that transport you to a genteel time. And if you're drawn to the great outdoors, the log and country-style homes in chapter three are homes where front porch living is blissfully serene. The last chapter explores contemporary homes, many in the Arts and Crafts style, where porches and sunrooms are dressed in nature-inspired woods, stones, and rich jewel tones.

No matter what style of home you live in, a few simple touches can color your front porch with class, charm, and comfort. Within these pages you will find useful advice and inspiring photographs to help you create your dream porch. The front porch is your home's harbor—a calming place between two worlds that allows you to express your love of beauty and the heartfelt value you place on hospitality.

Above: BECAUSE SO MANY ADULTS SPEND WORKDAYS AT A COMPUTER AND THE AVERAGE CHILD WATCHES TELEVISION THREE HOURS A DAY, MANY FAMILIES APPRECIATE THE CHANCE TO UNWIND, UNPLUG, AND VISIT FACE TO FACE IN THE COMFORTING EMBRACE OF THE FRONT PORCH. THE VAST SIZE OF THIS WRAPAROUND PORCH PROVIDES MANY OPPORTUNITIES FOR DINING, NAPPING, OR JUST SPENDING TIME TOGETHER.

WELCOMING PORCHES OF THE ROMANTIC-STYLE HOME

The Neoclassical taste that prevailed throughout the late eighteenth and early nineteenth centuries began to wane in popularity after the war of 1812 and the fall of Napoleon. As the nineteenth century progressed, the rising middle class rejected many aspects of Neoclassicism, and sought inspiration in the styles of the more recent past. The result was a revival of several "Romantic" styles. Three of the most appealing Romantic designs included the Greek Revival, the Gothic Revival, and the Italianate. Many of these homes survive today, offering elegant possibilities for front porch decor.

The Greek Revival was the first and perhaps the most popular of the Romantic styles. Americans admired it for its stately white columns reminiscent of ancient Greek temples, and for the Greek ideals of democracy that it represented. Greek Revival homes can feature small porticoes—entry porches that surround and shelter the front door—or sweeping, columned porches that extend across the home's facade.

One of the most picturesque of the revival styles was Gothic Revival, which features steeply pitched roofs and narrow, arched windows. This architectural style was inspired by medieval French and English church designs. Suitable for stone castles, large country homes, and even timber cottages, the Gothic Revival style also features one-story porches that are supported by Gothic arches.

From 1840 through 1880, Italianate architecture became increasingly popular. Hallmarks of this style

Opposite: A MAGNIFICENT EXAMPLE OF GREEK REVIVAL ARCHITECTURE, THIS MAJESTIC PORCH COULD WELCOME ROYALTY. THE GREEK REVIVAL STYLE WAS EXTREMELY POPULAR IN AMERICA FROM ABOUT 1830 THROUGH 1860, APPEARING ON PUBLIC BUILDINGS AND THROUGHOUT MANY STATE CAPITALS.

include: a low-pitched roof with overhanging eaves and decorative brackets; tall, narrow windows with arches; and small entry porches or full-width designs.

To help you add the timeless elegance of the Romantic porch or portico to your home, here are a few inspiring ideas from a variety of manufacturers and home designers.

Paint manufacturers such as the Sherwin-Williams Company offer a reproduction palette of colors—historically accurate shades for various architectural styles. The dominant colors for Greek Revival facades include white or cream. While columns are typically painted white, shutters are usually black. Appropriate colors for windowframes and doorways include neutral beiges or tans. For the Gothic Revival or Italianate home, a combination of subdued earthy shades are favored, such as greens, tans, browns, grays, and reds.

Two kinds of exterior paints are available and both work well on porches. Latex paint, which mixes with water, is very durable. Oil-based or alkyd paints work best in areas subject to high moisture or use. Generally, it's best to buy top-of-the-line paints with high percentages of binders (resins) and pigments, as these will help counter harmful UV rays which can fade paint. Better paints also promote adhesion and "breathability," the ability to resist blistering caused by moisture. A variety of stains can also provide solid protection for textured wood walls and floors.

For lighting, wrought-iron or black-glazed aluminum lanterns or brass wall sconces blend well with the formal styling of the Romantic porch. For accent lighting, experts often recommend recessed fixtures, which can be mounted inside a porch eave or overhang. Remember, lights that are exposed to the elements must be rated to withstand moisture.

If your front porch is screened or totally enclosed with glazed inserts, you can achieve an opulently authentic window treatment by layering shades, elegant draperies, and valances. To let in the sun, the draperies can be pulled back with tassel or rosette tiebacks. Other romantic choices include graceful balloon shades and swags in gold, blue, green, teal, rose, brown, or cream silks or velvets. Balloon swags featuring brass tiebacks elegantly crown the Romantic window while drawing attention to the view beyond the glass.

For open and screened porches, experts recommend a wide variety of textured flooring choices, such as mottled earth tone slate or granite dimension stone, or marble or terra-cotta tiles. A fitting touch for the floor of the enclosed Romantic porch is an elaborate oriental rug or floral Chinese needlepoint rug.

Furnishings that lend charm and personality to the Romantic-style porch include Rococo Revival-style cast-iron chairs and garden benches. Other historically accurate touches include teak or mahogany benches and chairs with scrolled armrests and finials, and graceful garden benches crafted from stone. Wicker also has its place on the Romantic porch, as some architectural scholars consider Italianate and Gothic Revival homes to be part of the early Victorian school of design.

Because the Romantic style is a classic look that calls to mind the grandeur of ancient or medieval periods, it's appropriate to fill the front porch with charming reminders of the past. Examples of fitting Romantic accessories for the porch and sunroom include garden statues of mythical gods and goddesses, gargoyles, animals, or angels; lush greenery perched on marble or stone pedestals; striped fabric cushions and pillows in neutral shades or vibrant golds, reds, blues, teals, roses, and greens; terra-cotta and cast stone planters filled with flowers; wrought-iron plant stands and hanging flower baskets; topiary trees; delicate floral swags with trailing vines for the front door; and for the ceiling, attractive and functional paddle fans to circulate the air and help keep insects away.

Above: THE ELEGANT WHITE COLUMNS ADD A TOUCH OF SOPHISTICATION AND CLASSICAL STYLE

TO THIS OTHERWISE SIMPLE PORCH.

Opposite: THE EXPANSIVE FRONT PORCH OF THIS LOVELY ITALIANATE HOME OFFERS A PLACE TO SIT AND MARVEL AT THE GLORIES OF THE BLUE SKY AND LUSH, PASTORAL SURROUNDINGS. **Right:** CLASSIC BLACK SHUTTERS AND PORCH FURNISHINGS, WHICH INCLUDE A BENCH, ROCKING CHAIR, AND PORCH SWING MADE MORE COMFORTABLE WITH THE ADDITION OF DUSTY ROSE PILLOWS, PROVIDE AN ELEGANT CONTRAST TO THE WHITE FACADE OF THIS ROMANTIC HOME. THE RICHLY TEXTURED MOSAIC STONE FLOOR, COLORFUL PILLOWS, AND SUSPENDED FLOWER BASKETS SEEM TO REFLECT THE SPRINGTIME AWAKENING OF THE SURROUNDING WOODS.

Right: CAREFREE AND CASUAL, THIS ROMANTICALLY STYLED FRONT PORCH PROVIDES A STRESS-FREE HAVEN FOR OVER-SCHEDULED FAMILIES. BRIGHTLY CHECKED ACCESSORIES AND COMFY WICKER FURNISHINGS OFFER DOWN-HOME EASE, WHILE SEVERAL PLANTERS BRING NATURE CLOSE.

Above left: THE FRONT PORCH AND SECOND-STORY SLEEPING PORCH OF THIS GRACIOUS GREEK REVIVAL HOME IN ST. FRANCISVILLE, LOUISIANA, ARE PERFECT GATHERING SPOTS FOR SHARING LEMONADE OR MINT JULEPS AND LEISURELY SOUTHERN HOSPITALITY. ST. FRANCISVILLE IS RENOWNED FOR ITS BEAUTIFULLY PRESERVED ANTEBELLUM PLANTATIONS. **Above right:** A CLOSER VIEW FROM THE HOME'S SLEEPING PORCH REVEALS A SPECTACULAR ROCKING CHAIR VIEW—AN AVENUE OF FLOWERING TREES AMID CAREFULLY TENDED GARDENS.

Above: A SLATE GRAY FLOOR WAS USED ON THIS ROMANTIC-STYLE PORCH TO GIVE THE SPACE A COOL SOPHISTICATION, WHICH IS SOFTENED BY A GENEROUS SUPPLY OF BRIGHT FLOWERS, BOTH IN THE BOX MOUNTED ON THE PORCH RAILING AND ON THE GORGEOUS BLOOMING SHRUB.

Opposite: THIS AIRY PORCH OFFERS A BEAUTIFUL VIEW OF THE NEARBY BAY. THOSE WHO VISIT IT CAN ENJOY BOTH THE SCENERY AND THE REFRESHING BREEZES THAT BLOW IN FROM THE WATER. **Above:** THE FRONT PORCH HAS LONG BEEN A SACRED HIDEAWAY WHERE GENERATIONS GATHER TO SHARE STORIES OF LONG AGO AND TO WATCH PARADES, DANCING FIREFLIES, AND LUMINOUS MOONS. **Right:** HERE'S A RARE SIGHT: AN UNOCCUPIED ROCKER IN THE SHADE OF A GREEK REVIVAL PORCH. MANY NINETEENTH-CENTURY PHYSICIANS BELIEVED ROCKING CHAIRS TO BE THERAPEUTIC, OFTEN REFERRING TO THEM AS "DIGESTIVE CHAIRS."

Above: LIKE STATELY WHITE TREE TRUNKS, IONIC COLUMNS ARE A SIGNIFI-CANT FEATURE OF THIS ROMANTIC GREEK REVIVAL HOME. HERE, A CURTAIN OF HANGING FLOWER BASKETS AND A ROW OF WINDOW BOXES ENLIVEN THE FRONT PORCH WITH COLOR AND FRAGRANCE. **Left:** IRELAND'S EMERALD GREEN LANDSCAPE ENCIRCLES THIS ROMANTIC HOME'S FRONT PORCH, ACCENTED BY FLOWERS, TRELLISES, AND CLASSIC STATUES. HERE, A GENTLE SCULPTED BOY BIDS "A HUNDRED THOUSAND WELCOMES" TO ALL WHO VISIT.

Right: THE EXPANSIVE PORCH AND GARDENS OF THIS HOME CREATE A GRAND SETTING FOR AFTERNOON TEAS, GRADUATION PARTIES, AND WEDDING RECEPTIONS. CLASSIC TOUCHES SUCH AS AN ORNATE BIRDBATH, POTTED FLOWERS ON THE PORCH STAIRS, AND THE DECORATIVE IRON RAILING LEADING TO THE PORCH ARE TESTIMONY TO THE OWNERS' PENCHANT FOR ELEGANCE.

Opposite: THE DELICATELY FLOWERED TABLECLOTH AND CHAIR CUSHIONS ECHO THE REAL BLOSSOMS AND THOSE IN THE ELEGANT RAILING TO CREATE A LOVELY CORNER IN WHICH TO RELAX. **Above left:** IT MAY BE 101 DEGREES IN THE SUN, BUT THIS PORCH'S RUSTIC BLUE SHUTTERS AND DOOR ADD A COOLING EFFECT, WHILE WARM PINK BLOSSOMS INFUSE TEXTURE AND VISUAL EXCITEMENT. **Above right:** IN THE SANCTUARY OF THIS SHELTERED ROMANTIC PORTICO, BALANCE AND BEAUTY ARE ACHIEVED THROUGH EARTHY COLORS, STUCCO AND STONE TEXTURES, AND LEAFY PATTERNS. THE ORNATE CAST-IRON CHAIR IS AN IDEAL CHOICE BECAUSE OF ITS TIMELESS DIGNITY AND GRACE.

Left: THE DECORATIVE ARCHED WINDOWS OF THIS GOTHIC REVIVAL PORTICO TAKE THEIR INSPIRATION FROM MEDIEVAL FRENCH AND ENGLISH CHURCH DESIGNS. THIS PORTICO IS ENCLOSED TO PROTECT VISITORS AND AN ARRAY OF COLORFUL PLANTS FROM INCLEMENT WEATHER.

Right: FULLY ENCLOSED PORTI-COES OFFER YEAR-ROUND SHELTER FOR GUESTS WHO COME CALLING, AS WELL AS A PLACE TO PUT DELICATE WICKER CHAIRS AND FOR SUN-LOVING PLANTS TO THRIVE.

Gracious Victorian Verandas and Conservatories

Bedecked with ornate furniture, a profusion of blooms, and old-fashioned fabrics and accessories, the decorative Victorian front porch is a portrait of a home in its "Sunday Best."

What makes the Victorian interpretation of the front porch or veranda so appealing is the careful attention paid to detail. On typical Victorian homes, there is an abundance of intricate woodwork—ornamental balustrades (two parallel rails held in place by posts with the space between filled with balusters that are scrolled, turned, or squared); decorative porch supports; roof brackets in the shape of vines, floral displays, or curvilinear designs; and delicate under-porch latticework. Four of the most stunning Victorian architectural styles that often feature expansive verandas are Stick, Queen Anne, Shingle, and Folk Victorian styles.

Stick-style homes generally have wooden shingles that are accentuated by patterns of horizontal, vertical, or diagonal boards or "stickwork." The quintessential Victorian home, the Queen Anne, can feature bay windows, projecting pavilions, towers, turrets, tall chimneys, patterned shingles, an encircling veranda, and sometimes, a second-story porch—perfect for sleeping outdoors under a blanket of stars. The Shingle-style home is aptly named, as its complex shape is covered with stained or painted shingles. And the Folk Victorian home features a simple Victorian design and a front porch graced with gingerbread trims.

Whether your home is a grand old Victorian or a newer home with "Gilded Age" touches, there are several elements of design you can bring in that will help you capture the nostalgic essence of the Victorian veranda.

Opposite: Like a delicate cream-colored rose on a white-frosted cake, this Folk Victorian home stands out in every season. Engaging porch features include traditional turned spindles and flat, jigsaw-cut balustrades and trim.

Porches need reflected light in order to be bright enough to function as outdoor living spaces. In the Victorian era, natural lighting was enhanced by painting the porch ceiling a sky blue or in some cases, repeating the pastel body color of the home. Porch floors were generally painted a moderate gray or green to camouflage dust and dirt.

Ornate wrought-iron or brass fixtures are at home on the classic Victorian porch. For after-dark dining and entertaining, vintage oil lamps cast a warm glow.

Victorian front porches readily employed striped canvas awnings to shade the front of the home, and to provide added comfort and privacy. Today, porch awnings can be found in a variety of sizes, colors, and designs (some of which can be automatically extended or retracted at the push of a button).

Simple sisal and Japanese tatami mats can provide texture and color on Victorian porch floors. Other popular summer floor covering choices are rag rugs, or in an enclosed porch area, Oriental rugs.

Wicker furniture brings curvaceous designs, exotic texture, and romance to the veranda. Wildly popular during the Victorian era, wicker furnishings are woven from rattan, willow, straw, rush, raffia, palm, spun wood pulp, buri, or bamboo. Manufacturers have created synthetic willow furnishings that can stand up to the elements much better than antique wicker, which is ideally suited for enclosed spaces.

Some other furnishing ideas for the Victorian porch include cast-iron chairs, tables, and benches; wooden rockers, gliders, and trunks; and vintage ice-cream parlor tables and chairs. For homeowners who enjoy an afternoon siesta, here's some welcome news. Yesterday's rigid rope hammock has been improved. Today you can find a wide range of comfortable hammocks available in synthetic mesh, nylon net, quilted material, woven Mayan fabric, and more. The hammock was a beloved prop of the Victorian era, and it makes a nice touch on your period porch.

The Victorian passion for flowers shines through when the porch is adorned with wire plant stands, terra-cotta pots, or painted wheelbarrows all filled to the brim with fragrant posies. Other vintage touches include pillows and cushions in floral chintz, stripes, ginghams, and plaids; white lace, linen, or crocheted tablecloths; tea time china settings; decorative quilts; straw hats; and decoratively painted watering cans.

Today's elegant glass-enclosed conservatory dates back to eighteenth-century Europe, where "orangeries" were built to protect citrus trees from the elements.

Linda Krapf of Casa Del Sol in Long Valley, New Jersey, an authority on state-of-the-art Amdega & Machin Conservatories from Great Britain says, "Conservatories are a celebration of light and in Great Britain, they're a matter of sanity. They nourish the part of our souls that needs to see the drama of the outdoors all year round."

In the last decade, many North Americans have enlarged their homes with a conservatory, which is typically added adjacent to the kitchen, living room, or family room. Some people even have conservatories built onto the front of their homes as a surprising yet sophisticated alternative to the traditional front porch. Conservatory designs can range from the simple to the breathtakingly ornate.

Below: The front porches of several quaint wood-framed cottages in Martha's Vineyard, Massachusetts, entice with colorful antique wicker and glorious blooms in hanging baskets.

Left: AN ORNATE WICKER CHAIR TAKES ITS RIGHTFUL PLACE ON THE FRONT PORCH OF A RESTORED 1890 VICTORIAN FARMHOUSE. A LEGACY OF THE VICTORIAN ERA, WICKER IS EQUALLY AT HOME ON ROMANTIC, RUSTIC, ARTS AND CRAFTS, AND CONTEMPORARY PORCHES. **Above:** THE VIEW FROM THE WRAPAROUND PORCH OF THIS SHINGLE-STYLE VICTORIAN COTTAGE IN COASTAL NEW ENGLAND IS BREATHTAKING. THE SEASIDE HOME WAS BUILT IN 1896 BY ARCHITECT WILLIAM EMERSON FOR LANDSCAPE ARCHITECT FREDERICK LAW OLMSTED.

Left: THE VICTORIANS WERE GREAT BELIEVERS IN THE INVIGORATING BENEFITS OF FRESH AIR AND OFTEN SLEPT OUTDOORS ON SECOND-STORY PORCHES ON SUMMER NIGHTS. THE SLEEPING PORCH OF THIS HOME IS ALL DECKED OUT IN ITS GINGERBREAD TRIM, AND IT NO DOUBT PROVIDED A SEASIDE RESPITE FROM CITY AIR AND DREADED TUBERCULOSIS AT THE TURN OF THE CENTURY. **Opposite:** THE FRONT PORCH OF THIS VICTORIAN HOME MAKES A FRIENDLY FIRST IMPRESSION WITH GREGARIOUS GERANIUMS, EVER-READY ROCKERS, AND FRESHLY PAINTED BALUSTERS AND DECORATIVE PORCH SUPPORTS.

Left: During autumn's golden days, the front porch of this Victorian home offers the perfect vantage point for watching the shimmering reflection of the surrounding maple and birch trees on the surface of a nearby lake.

Below: SISAL OR COIR MATS ARE A WELCOME ADDITION ON THE FRONT PORCH AND ARE TYPICAL OF VICTORIAN-STYLE PORCHES. THEY'RE MADE OF NATURAL FIBERS AND CAN EASILY BE SWEPT CLEAN.

Above: THE WRAPAROUND PORCH OF THIS SEASIDE VICTORIAN HOME ENCHANTS WITH ITS STRIKING COBALT BLUE SHUTTERS, WARM RED AND GOLD POTTED FLOWERS, AND HANDSOME WOODEN FURNITURE.

Opposite: Dazzling tropical birds and butterflies are just a few of nature's treasures that can be enjoyed from the vantage of this wraparound veranda. A gem of architectural design, this porch captures the essence of Victorian embellishment with lace-like brackets, spindlework porch supports, and a decorative frieze.

Above: A graceful balustrade, spindlework porch supports, patterned wood shingles, and classic wicker unite to create the picture of Victorian grandeur at this home. **Right:** This Victorian home engages the eye with its carefully orchestrated symphony of colors, architectural designs, and textures. The enormous front porch provides a wonderful spot for dining, sipping lemonade, or catching up with an old friend.

Opposite: THIS LOVELY HOME USES FAVORITE CLASSICAL DESIGN ELEMENTS, SUCH AS THE GREEK KEY MOTIF AND THE ON-POINT CHECKERED WALK-WAY, TO WONDERFUL EFFECT. **Above:** SOME VICTORIAN EXTERIORS ARE DRESSED IN UP TO THREE, FOUR, OR FIVE DIFFERENT COLORS, MAKING HOME UPKEEP AN EXPENSIVE BUT WORTHWHILE LABOR OF LOVE. THIS PORCH HAS BEEN PAINSTAKINGLY PAINTED, EACH COMPONENT A DIFFERENT COLOR.

Opposite: YESTERDAY'S GLASS-ENCLOSED VICTORIAN CONSERVATORY, LIKE THE FRONT PORCH, IS ENJOYING A WELL-DESERVED REVIVAL. CONSERVATORIES ARE PERFECT FOR CASUAL BREAKFASTS OR FORMAL ENTERTAINING AMID ORCHIDS, POTTED PALMS, LILIES, AND SPLASHING FOUNTAINS. HERE, FLORAL PILLOWS PAY TRIBUTE TO THE SYMPHONY OF COLOR AND FRAGRANCE IN THIS MINIATURE GARDEN OF EDEN. **Above:** THE NINETEENTH-CENTURY PASSION FOR GARDENING IS ALIVE AND WELL IN THIS VICTORIAN SETTING. A FEW OF THE PERIOD ACCENTS SHOWCASED ON THE PORCH INCLUDE THE WICKER SETTEE, MISMATCHED FLORAL PILLOWS, THE PRIVACY SCREEN, A STRAW HAT, AN ASSORTMENT OF BASKETS, AND BUNCHES OF DRIED FLOWERS.

Rustic and Country-Style Porches

If you love the warmth and character of log homes, you're in good company. Each year, more and more people choose to build or restore a log house. Homeowners choose log homes not only for their natural appearance, but for their creative designs, low maintenance, and energy efficiency.

Country-style homes are also extremely popular because they remind us of our close kinship with the land and the days when home and hearth were crafted by hand. Typical country-style facades feature simple, natural building materials such as wood, stone, and brick. Some common exterior elements include dormers, arched windows, sturdy chimneys, and rambling porches, often dressed up with Victorian gingerbread trims. The mood of the country-style home is warm, comfortable, and unpretentious. Inside and out, it celebrates natural materials, simple handmade furnishings, and warm colors. Often, country-style homes emphasize regional styles such as Southwestern or Adirondack, or furnishings and accessories crafted locally.

Barbara Martin, Executive Director of The Log Homes Council of the National Association of Homebuilders says, "Log homes exude a warm, soothing environment that provides a sense of permanence and solid construction." Many styles of log homes exist today, ranging from the traditional Appalachian to the country farmhouse to the contemporary. They're constructed of indigenous woods such as oak, cypress, or a native variety of cedar or pine. The front porch is an important amenity to the log home: it protects the home's facade from extreme weather conditions while providing a bright outdoor living space.

The Log Homes Council recommends that you follow the home maintenance schedule provided by the company that builds your log home. (See Sources to get more information on maintaining your log home.)

To achieve a rustic look, hang wrought-iron lanterns by the front door to add the perfect pioneering accent, or choose wall sconces fashioned from wrought iron or brass. For tabletop lighting, handcrafted tin lanterns shimmer with gentle radiance.

Opposite: Not all rustic homes are fashioned from timber logs. This wood shingle dwelling celebrates a more refined country style with its antique-laden front porch. There's ample room for casual dining and basking in the glow of a field of radiant sunflowers.

On the screened or enclosed porch, matchstick or bamboo blinds can be hung, or weatherproofed acrylic fabric curtains and matching pillows can be sewn to add color and privacy. For country-style homes, charming window treatments include plaid, striped, and gingham curtains, flowery chintzes, toiles de Jouy, and candlewick, a natural toned cotton with delicate embroidery.

Bright braided rag rugs or primitive hooked rugs offer a homey welcome. Other popular floor covering choices include hand-stenciled coir mats (coir is the stiff outer fiber on a coconut husk). They're weather durable and can be easily cleaned with a whisk broom.

Hand-me-down garden furniture, wicker, or old painted wooden pieces can comfortably outfit the front porch of log and country-style homes. Another down-to-earth choice is the rustic Adirondack chair, invented around 1900, which features a wide sloped back, an inclined seat, and wide arms.

Perhaps the most exquisite way to bring nature's textures onto the porch is to decorate with vintage or reproduction rustic furniture. Since the late 1800s, rustic furniture has been handcrafted from branches, stumps, and twigs. Some antique pieces are now considered folk art or natural sculpture, and they can be worth hundreds or even thousands of dollars.

Several unique styles of antique and newly created rustic furniture can be found today through antique dealers, individual builders, and through a handful of manufacturers. Popular types of rustic furnishings include: Adirondack or "Northwoods," Appalachian or "Southern Root and Twig," Amish, Gypsy, Indiana Hickory, Antler and Horn, and Western.

Invite birds and butterflies to drop by your porch with fragrant flower baskets, blossoming windowboxes, and a hummingbird feeder or two. Soften rough-hewn chairs with smooth pillows and cushions done in plaids, ginghams, stripes, floral chintzes, Native American designs, or wildlife prints. And if you like, display old outdoor collectibles such as wooden decoys, lobster traps, snowshoes, skis, fishing rods, and baskets, all ideal accent pieces. Simple graniteware pitchers or twig baskets filled with fresh or dried flowers will add color and design. Handcarved primitive animals or birds are another folksy, rustic accent.

Opposite: A parade of impatiens and other blooms surround this country home's front porch, making it the center of attention for all who visit.

Opposite: FAR FROM THE NOISE OF CITY TRAFFIC, THIS RUSTIC PORCH SOOTHES THE SPIRIT WITH NATURE'S RHAPSODY OF CRICKETS, LOONS, AND GENTLE BREEZES. EVEN THE TINIEST OF PORCHES CAN MAKE ROOM FOR HOSPITALITY WITH A FEW COMFY CHAIRS FOR WATCHING NATURE'S LIGHT SHOWS. **Above:** SYMBOLIC OF THE PIONEERING SPIRIT, THE LOG HOME HAS TIMELESS APPEAL. **Right:** HANDMADE RUSTIC FURNITURE ADDS AN AUTHENTIC LOOK TO THE LOG HOME PORCH. THE ADDITION OF VIVID RED, GREEN, YELLOW, OR BLUE PATTERNED PILLOWS OR CUSHIONS WOULD KINDLE VISUAL EXCITEMENT AND SOFTEN THE ENDEARING ROUGH EDGES OF THE SCENE.

Left: THE NATURAL CHARACTER OF THIS COUNTRY PORCH'S PLANK FLOOR CAN BE PRESERVED WITH THE APPLICATION OF A TRANSLUCENT WOOD STAIN, PROTECTED BY SEVERAL COATINGS OF CLEAR VARNISH.

Opposite left: BECAUSE SO MANY RUSTIC HOMES ARE BUILT IN WOODED AREAS, MANY PEOPLE SCREEN THEIR FRONT PORCHES TO KEEP OUT INSECTS AS WELL AS CHIPMUNKS, RACCOONS, SQUIRRELS, SKUNKS, OPOSSUMS, AND OTHER CURIOUS CRITTERS. **Opposite right:** BRIGHT YELLOW FLOWERS, A CHEERFUL PLAID BLANKET, AND HONEY-HUED ROCKERS ILLUMINATE THE NATURAL WOOD AND STONE OF THIS COUNTRY PORCH. A WROUGHT-IRON LANTERN, PRIMITIVE BASKETS, AN OLD WATERING CAN, AND A BUTTER CHURN PLAY SUPPORTING ROLES IN CREATING A SETTING THAT MIRRORS A DISTANT, SIMPLER ERA.

Opposite bottom: CAMP-STYLE ADIRONDACK CHAIRS HAVE BEEN A REVERED PORCH FURNISHING SINCE THE TURN OF THE CENTURY. A BEACON OF HOSPITALITY, THESE HARDY CHAIRS CAN BE STAINED OR PAINTED ANY COLOR TO ADD SUBTLE OR BOLD CHARM TO PORCH SETTINGS.

Opposite: THIS SPACIOUS DECK HAS BEEN STRIPPED OF MOST OF ITS SUMMER FURNISHINGS IN PREPARATION FOR A HARSH MOUNTAIN WINTER. STORING PORCH AND DECK FURNITURE IN A WARM, DRY ENVIRONMENT EVERY AUTUMN WILL HELP MAINTAIN ITS BEAUTY AND STRENGTH FOR YEARS TO COME. **Above left:** THE RUSSET RED OF THE BRICK FLOOR COMPLEMENTS THE DEEP WOODEN TONES OF THE ANTIQUE TABLE AND ROCKER ON THIS PORCH, CREATING A SIMPLE YET STRIKING SETTING FOR FRESH-AIR DINING. **Above right:** THE RUGGED NATURAL BEAUTY OF THE LOG HOME PORCH IS ENHANCED WHEN BRIGHTLY COLORED ACCESSORIES ARE CHOSEN FOR TABLE SETTINGS AND FURNISHINGS. HERE, THE RAPPORT OF TRANQUIL BLUES, CRISP YELLOWS, AND VIBRANT REDS HEIGHTEN THE SPLENDOR OF THE MOUNTAIN VISTA WHILE ENHANCING THE COMFORT OF THE PORCH SETTING.

Above: THIS CONTEMPORARY LOG HOME PORCH OFFERS THE BEST SEAT IN THE HOUSE FOR WATCHING NATURE'S CHANGING KALEIDOSCOPE OF COLORS. MODERN WROUGHT-IRON RAILINGS AND AN UPDATED RUSTIC CHAIR AND BENCH ADD DRAMA AND COMFORT, WHILE THE PADDLE FAN CIRCULATES SUMMER BREEZES AND HELPS KEEP INSECTS AWAY.

Right: IN THE SHADE OF THE ENCIRCLING WOODS, THIS RUSTIC HOME'S BRIGHT, PAINTED RAILING LIGHTS UP THE HOME'S FACADE WITH A WARM RED SHADE THAT PLAYS OFF THE GERANIUMS ON THE PORCH.

Above: THIS COUNTRY-STYLE PORCH ACTS AS A DECORATIVE FRAME FOR NATURE'S PRICELESS MASTERPIECES. EACH SEASON UNVEILS NEW TREASURES, FROM SPRING'S FIRST CROCUSES TO SUMMER'S BLACK-EYED SUSANS; AND FROM AUTUMN'S FIERY MAPLES TO WINTER'S SNOWFLAKE BALLET.

ARTS AND CRAFTS AND CONTEMPORARY PORCHES AND SUNROOMS

From about 1905 through 1920, one of the most popular home designs was the Craftsman, which was built to harmonize with the landscape in "colors that please and cheer." This simplified style was one of the first examples of twentieth-century architectural modernism. Its inspiration came from the British and American Arts and Crafts Movements, which favored honest craftsmanship over mass production and function and warmth over revivalism and embellishment.

Identifying features of the Craftsman home include rustic building materials such as wood and cobblestones, a low-pitched gabled roof with wide overhanging eaves, and a front porch with tapered square columns resting on massive piers. The bungalow, a one-story home with a deep, cozy porch, is also rooted in the Arts and Crafts Movement. It was the most fashionable style in America from the turn of the century through 1940.

After World War II, several sleek contemporary styles of homes became popular, such as the Ranch style and the Split-Level. At the same time, contemporary versions of traditional favorites such as the Victorian and the French Eclectic home also sprang up, providing homeowners with the latest in building materials and energy-efficient designs.

Whether you live in a rustic Arts and Crafts bungalow or a stunning contemporary home, here are a few tips that will help you create an ambience of comfort and memorable style for your front porch.

Traditional Arts and Crafts colors for home exteriors include such earth tones as olive green, clay orange, tan-brown, terra-cotta red, stone gray, and sand yellow. Arts and Crafts porch ceiling colors include blue and heather gray. For contemporary homes, a spectrum of color choices exist, including bright, neutral, and pastel shades.

Opposite: THE PORCH OF THIS ARTS AND CRAFTS BUNGALOW WAS DESIGNED TO SERVE AS A GENTLE BRIDGE BETWEEN THE SURROUNDING COUNTRYSIDE AND THE SANCTUARY OF THE HOME.

Popular Arts and Crafts lighting fixtures include Japanese lanterns featuring a gridlike copper frame, brass sconces, and Victorian or Edwardian fixtures. In the contemporary home, recessed lighting fixtures are ideal on the front porch or in the sunroom. Also noteworthy for outdoor use are high-tech marine-style bulkhead lights with wire cages.

Translucent stained glass and leaded glass windows are striking features that lend drama to the front porch of many Arts and Crafts style homes. These windows need no dressing, as that would be gilding the lily. Effective window treatments for the contemporary sunporch include simple wooden shutters, natural-colored bamboo shades, or matchstick blinds.

Arts and Crafts and contemporary homes reflect the beauty of nature by readily employing wood, stone, and natural fibers in their decor. Excellent choices for the porch floor are stained or painted wood flooring; ceramic tiles in natural colors or faux finishes (simulated marble, granite, wood grains, etc.); and dimension stones such as slate, marble, and granite. For the sunroom porch floor, any kind of natural floor covering can be complemented by sisal or coir mats or Oriental- or William Morris–style rugs. Morris founded the English Arts and Crafts Movement and established a workshop that produced handcrafted furniture, carpeting, wallpaper, and textiles in celebrated floral and Gothic designs.

To add natural comfort to the contemporary-style porch, key choices include wicker or wooden chairs, rockers, settees, and tables. For an authentic Arts and Crafts touch, vintage or reproduction Mission oak furnishings lend charm and simplicity.

The Arts and Crafts or contemporary porch or sunroom can be dressed in muted jewel tones that suggest balance and serenity. Some key colors to use include reds, greens, roses, golds, and blues. Other classic touches include handcrafted pottery, hammered copper sconces, William Morris–style tapestry pillows, Southwestern or Mediterranean inspired pillows or rugs, Oriental china vases filled with wildflowers, terra-cotta planters, and simple saltglaze crocks.

Opposite: A WIDE ARRAY OF MODERN FURNISHINGS IN WOOD, SYNTHETIC WICKER, CAST ALUMINUM, OR WROUGHT-IRON CAN IMPART AN UPBEAT ATTITUDE ON THE CONTEMPORARY PORCH. **Above:** THE DOMED CEILING LIGHT FIXTURES AND SIMPLE ROUNDED COLUMNS BRING A TOUCH OF CLASSICAL STYLE TO THIS LOVELY CONTEMPORARY PORCH.

Opposite: THIS UPDATED ARTS AND CRAFTS HOME OFFERS THE PERFECT PORCH LOOKOUT FOR SPECTACULAR SUNSETS AND FALLING STARS. ADIRONDACK CHAIRS COVERED WITH A FRESH COAT OF WHITE PAINT MAKE FOR A PLEASING SPOT TO REST AND TAKE IN THE VIEW. **Above:** WITH GRACE AND SIMPLICITY, THIS ARTS AND CRAFTS-STYLE HOME DOVETAILS WITH THE NATURAL REALM THROUGH ITS USE OF WOOD, STONES, AND EARTHEN COLORS. THE ORIENTAL LANTERN, THE RESPLENDENT STAINED GLASS DOOR, AND THE MISSION OAK BENCH ARE THREE HALLMARKS OF ARTS AND CRAFTS DECOR.

Above: A GRAND SETTING FOR A MIDSUMMER NIGHT'S SOIREE, THIS CONTEMPORARY HOME'S PORCHES BECKON WITH EXOTIC ARCHITECTURE, WICKER FURNISHINGS, AND SOFT, WARM LIGHTING. **Opposite:** THIS CONTEMPORARY HOME MAKES THE MOST OF SEVERAL TRIED AND TRUE PORCH TRADITIONS. GRACEFUL GRECIAN COLUMNS AND UNPRETENTIOUS BALUSTRADES, A PRACTICAL GRAY FLOOR, COMFORTABLE ROCKERS, AND TERRA-COTTA PLANTERS THAT ADD A SPLASH OF COLOR ALL WORK IN HARMONY TO CREATE A WELCOMING "HARBOR."

Left: Around the world, the cherished front porch is known by such musical sounding names as "veranda" (India and Great Britain), "piazza" (Italy), "portale" (Spain), and "galerie" (France). This beautiful piazza overlooks the coastline of Pantelleria Island, which is located near Sicily.

Right: Simple or decorative planters add visual interest, color, and texture to every front porch. Two excellent materials to look for include stone and clay. Quality cast stone containers can withstand cold temperatures and provide a home for moss and lichen, while clay pots feature a porous surface that helps absorb and distribute water.

Above: THE BLINDING WHITE STUCCO OF THIS CONTEMPORARY HOME'S PORCH IS SOFTENED BY NATURAL WOOD FURNISHINGS, PLANTS, AND EARTH-TONE WALL HANGINGS. **Right:** THIS EXTROVERTED MEDITERRANEAN BALCONY SETS THE STAGE FOR AN EVENING OF SUPERB CUISINE AND COMPANY. A CANOPY OF INTOXICATING HOT-PINK BOUGAINVILLEA BLOSSOMS, ALONG WITH VIVID PRIMARY COLOR TABLE SETTINGS AND CUSHIONS, DAZZLE THE SENSES.

Opposite: EVERYWHERE ON THIS SOUTH AMERICAN-INFLUENCED PORCH ARE OBJECTS OF GREAT BEAUTY. THE INTRICATELY CARVED PORCH COLUMNS, THE TILE FLOOR, DECORATIVE MIRRORS, BRIGHT PILLOWS AND BLANKET, WOODEN FURNISHINGS, NATIVE POTTERY, AND ABUNDANT PLANTS ALL WEAVE THEIR MAGIC TO CREATE A CAPTIVATING SETTING FOR RELAXATION AND ROMANCE. **Right:** THIS STUNNING SUNROOM WAS CREATED OUT OF A LONG, RAMBLING FRONT PORCH. THERE IS NOTHING COVERING THE WINDOWS—THEY ARE OPEN TO ALLOW THE OUTDOORS TO COME IN TO THE HOUSE.

Above: MANY HOUSES BEING CONSTRUCTED TODAY ARE SMALLER THAN THOSE BUILT IN THE NINETEENTH AND EARLY TWENTIETH CENTURIES, SO THE ADDITION OF A FRONT PORCH CAN PROVIDE A VITAL STRUCTURAL FACELIFT. **Opposite:** LIKE A BRIGHT WHITE CANVAS, THIS CONTEMPORARY PORCH COMES ALIVE WITH SPLASHES OF COLORFUL FLOWERS AND SIMPLE YET ELEGANT FURNISHINGS.

Above left: A BREEZY PORCH AND FLAGSTONE TERRACE PROVIDE CASUAL COMFORT AND STYLE IN THIS CONTEMPORARY SHINGLE HOME. SIMPLE WOODEN FURNISHINGS, COLONIAL LIGHTING FIXTURES, AND BRIGHT GREEN CUSHIONS UNITE BOTH OUTDOOR LIVING SPACES. **Above right:** MANY HOMEOWNERS HAVE TRANSFORMED THEIR OPEN FRONT PORCH TO A YEAR-ROUND SUNROOM. HERE, SIMPLE COUNTRY COMFORT IS ACHIEVED WITH WICKER, WOOD, AND ACCENTS OF CHEERY COLOR. **Opposite:** FRONT PORCHES ARE VALUED NOT ONLY FOR THEIR GOOD LOOKS AND TRADITION OF HOSPITALITY, BUT FOR THEIR ENERGY EFFICIENCY. THEY NOT ONLY PROTECT THE FACADE OF THE HOME FROM THE ELEMENTS, BUT CAN REDUCE AIR CONDITIONING EXPENSES BY SHELTERING THE HOME FROM THE SUN'S INTENSE RAYS.

Sources

FIXTURES AND FURNISHINGS

Adirondack Museum
P.O. Box 99
Route 30
Blue Mountain Lake, NY
12812
(518) 352-7311
*Has an annual rustic furniture
fair*

Brown Jordan
9860 Gidley Street
P.O. Box 5688
El Monte, CA 91734
(818) 443-8971
Porch and garden furnishings

Casablanca Fan Co.
761 Corporate Center Drive
Pomona, CA 91768
(888) 227-2178
Ceiling fans

Casa Del Sol
P.O. Box 680
Long Valley, NJ 07853
(908) 979-9400
Conservatories

Log Homes Council
(800) 368-5242
Log home maintenance

Old Hickory Furniture Co.
403 S. Noble Street
Shelbyville, IN 46176
(800) 232-2275
Rustic furniture

Sherwin-Williams Company
101 Prospect Avenue
Cleveland, OH 44115
(216) 566-2000
Paint

ARCHITECTS AND INTERIOR DESIGNERS

(pages 2, 10, 14, 19 left, 25,
26, 30-31)
Steve Smith, Preservation
Architect
Burlington, VT
(802) 863-2227

(pages 18, 35 left, 51 both,
64)
Kulhanek Construction
Los Angeles, CA
(310) 474-6722

(pages 31 right, 33, 36 left,
42)
John Silverio, architect
Lincolnville, ME
(207) 763-3885

(page 39)
Maryann Vandenburg,

renovator
Waterbury, CT
(203) 757-9901

(page 35)
Cindy Stentz, designer
Bellingham, WA
(360) 738-1597

(page 45)
Dale and Mary Haaland,
owners/designers
Bellingham, WA
(360) 733-3042

(pages 46, 48)
Theodore & Theodore,
architects
Dresden, ME
(207) 737-2131

(page 49 top left)
Bullock & Company Builders
Creekmore, Ontario
(705) 466-2505

(page 50)
Martin Kuckly, designer
New York, NY
(212) 772-2228

(page 52 top)
Bushman Dreyfus, architects
Charlottesville, VA
(804) 295-1936

(page 54)
Design Alliance, architects
Portland, ME
(207) 773-1756

(page 57)
Thom Rouselle, architect
Biddeford Pool, ME
(207) 282-6800

(page 59)
Greene & Greene, architects
Los Angeles, CA
(213) 874-4278

(page 61)
John Gillepsie, architect
Camden, ME
(207) 236-8054

(page 65)
John Cole Interiors
Los Angeles, CA
(310) 652-6288

(page 67)
Orcutt Associates, architects
Yarmouth, ME
(207) 846-7702

(page 68 left)
Kevin Kalman, Kalman
Construction
Nantucket, ME
(508) 228-5825

SOURCES

PHOTOGRAPHY CREDITS

©Philip Beaurline: p. 52 top (Bushman Dreyfus Architects)

©Grey Crawford: p. 65 (John Cole Interiors)

©Sandra Ellrich: pp. 21, 34, 52 bottom

FPG International: ©David Bartruff: p. 47 top; ©Ron Chapple: p. 56; ©Richard Gaul: p. 13; ©Mike Malyszko: p. 29; ©E. Alan McGee: p. 15 top; ©Frederick McKinney: pp. 19 right, 20 top, 36 right; ©Richard Nowitz: p. 32; ©Thayer Syme: p. 53

©Tria Giovan: pp. 6, 9, 15 bottom, 20 bottom, 23 right, 40, 41, 49 top right, 66

©Nancy Hill: p. 49 bottom (Sagamore Lodge, Raquet Lake, NY)

©John E. Kane: p. 39 (Marianna Vandenburgh, renovator)

©Tim Street-Porter: pp. 47 bottom (Shirley Ritts, designer), 59 (Greene & Greene, architects)

©Paul Rocheleau: pp. 16 both (Rosedown Estate, St. Francisville, LA), 17

©Eric Roth: p. 68 left (Kevin Kalman, Kalman Construction)

©Bill Rothschild: p. 50 (Martin Kuckly, designer)

©Angelo Tondini/Focus Team: pp. 60, 62 both, 63 both

©Mark Turner: pp. 35 right (Cindy Stentz, designer), 45 (Dale and Mary Haaland, owners/designers)

©Brian Vanden Brink: pp. 2, 10, 14, 19 left, 25, 26, 30-31 (Billings Farm, Woodstock, VT; Steve Smith, preservation architect), 31 right, 33, 36 left, 42 (John Silverio, architect), 46, 48 (Theodore & Theodore Architects), 49 top left (Bullock & Company Builders), 54 (Design Alliance, architects), 57 (Thom Rouselle, architect), 58 (John Silverio, architect), 61 (John Gillespie, architect), 67 (Orcutt Associates, architects), 68 right, 69 (Robert Currie Interior Design)

©Dominique Vorillion: pp. 18, 35 left, 51 both, 64 (Kulhanek Construction)

©Elizabeth Whiting Associates: pp. 22, 23 left, 24, 37, 38

INDEX